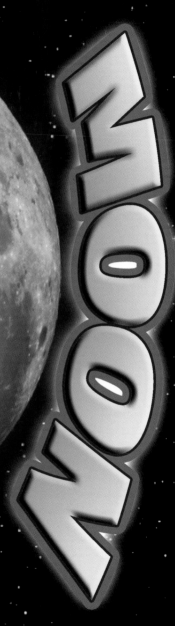

MOON

INSIDE OUTER SPACE

Julie K. Lundgren

rourke
Educational Media

rourkeeducationalmedia.com

Scan for Related Titles
and Teacher Resources

Teaching Focus:

Vocabulary: Find the words in the book that are related to science concepts. What do these science words mean?

Before Reading:

Building Academic Vocabulary and Background Knowledge

Before reading a book, it is important to set the stage for your child or student by using pre-reading strategies. This will help them develop their vocabulary, increase their reading comprehension, and make connections across the curriculum.

1. Read the title and look at the cover. *Let's make predictions about what this book will be about.*

2. Take a picture walk by talking about the pictures/photographs in the book. Implant the vocabulary as you take the picture walk. Be sure to talk about the text features such as headings, Table of Contents, glossary, bolded words, captions, charts/ diagrams, or Index.

3. Have students read the first page of text with you then have students read the remaining text.

4. Strategy Talk – use to assist students while reading.
   - Get your mouth ready
   - Look at the picture
   - Think…does it make sense
   - Think…does it look right
   - Think…does it sound right
   - Chunk it – by looking for a part you know

5. Read it again.

6. After reading the book complete the activities below.

Content Area Vocabulary

Use glossary words in a sentence.

atmosphere
axis
observatories
orbits
satellite
telescopes

After Reading:

Comprehension and Extension Activity

After reading the book, work on the following questions with your child or students in order to check their level of reading comprehension and content mastery.

1. *Which space mission was the first to go to the Moon?* (Summarize)
2. *How does the Hubble Space Telescope take pictures of the Moon?* (Asking questions)
3. *How does wind and rain affect a surface?* (Infer)
4. *How does the Moon glow?* (Asking questions)

Extension Activity

The Moon has no weather. There isn't any wind, snow, or rain to change the surface. Using this information, create a hypothesis about your footprint on Earth. Will the impression stay forever? Fill a bin with sand. Step onto the sand to leave your footprint. Keep this bin indoors away from any weather. Now go to the playground or sandbox and make a footprint. After several days look at the different footprints. What changed? Why were there changes in one and not the other?

Table of Contents

One Moon for Earth

Earth and seven other planets circle the Sun, the star in the center of our solar system. Earth has one natural **satellite**, our Moon.

Sun

Earth

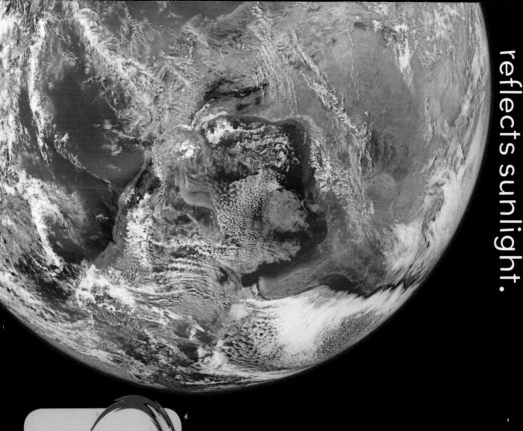

From Earth, the Moon appears to glow. But unlike a star, which makes its own light, the Moon only reflects sunlight.

The Moon is about one-fourth the size of Earth, similar to the difference between a softball and a basketball.

Many scientists think that the Moon formed when a giant meteor crashed into Earth and pieces zinged off into space.

Volcanoes and meteors have made the Moon's surface rocky and rough. No volcanoes are active on the Moon today.

About 238,000 miles (384,500 kilometers) separate the Moon and Earth.

Moon

Earth

Because the Moon has a thin **atmosphere**, it has no weather. Without wind or rain to wear away the Moon's surface, it does not change.

273°F
(134°C)

-243°F
(-153°C)

Without an atmosphere to blanket it, temperatures on the Moon may reach 273° Fahrenheit (134° Celsius) in sunlight and -243° Fahrenheit (-153° Celsius) in darkness.

Moon Motion

Like Earth, the Moon turns on its **axis**. It also **orbits** the Earth.

Because the Moon orbits Earth in about 27 days and turns on its axis in the same amount of time, the same side of the Moon faces Earth all the time.

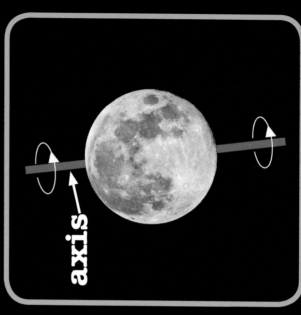

axis

The axis is an invisible line that can't be seen.

When viewing the full Moon, some say they can see what looks like a poodle in the Moon.

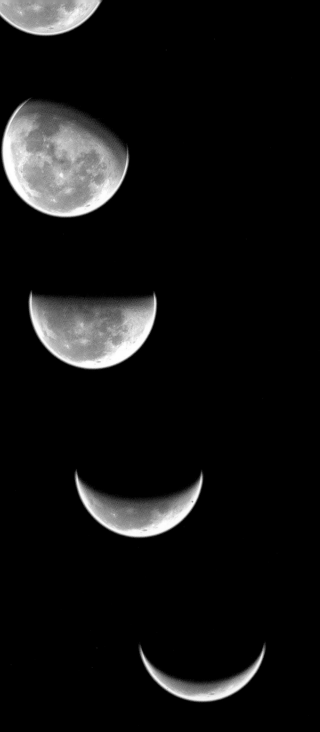

Sometimes only a slice of the Moon can be seen from Earth, while other times the Moon is full. Only the part of the Moon that is lit by the Sun is visible.

As the Moon orbits Earth, our view of it changes in a regular cycle.

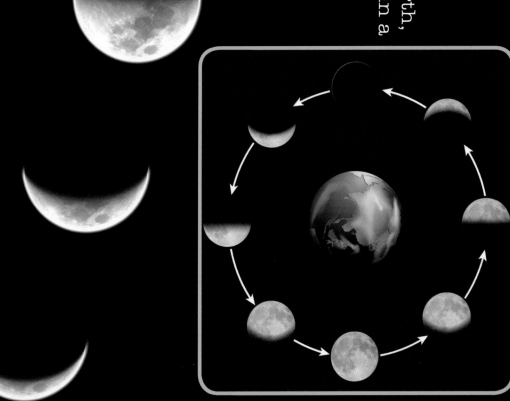

Usually, there is one full Moon in a month. But about every three years, two full Moons will appear in one month. The second one is called a blue Moon.

Fly Me to the Moon

The Moon has always sparked wonder.

Telescopes help scientists study the Moon

and other objects in space.

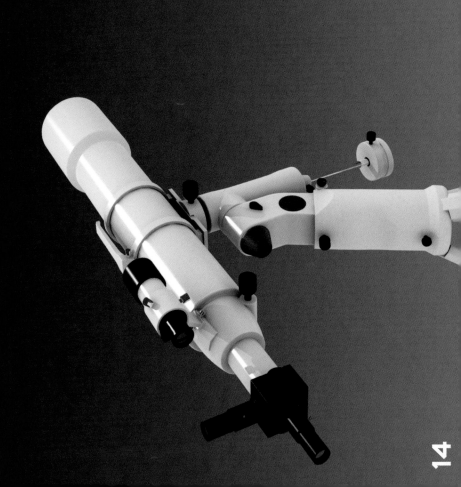

The best time to study the Moon is during its first quarter. When the Moon is in its first quarter, the Sun hits it at an angle. It creates shadows on the surface and more detail is visible.

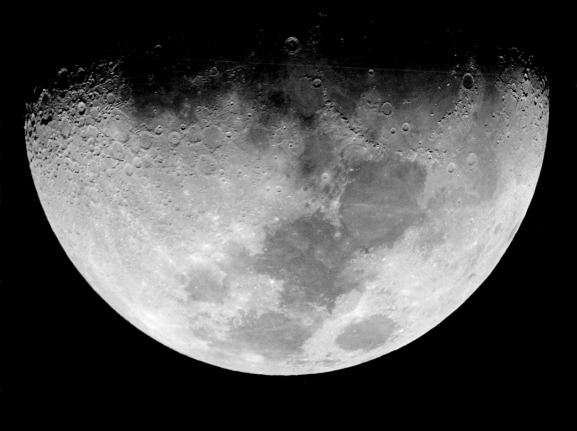

Scientists build large telescopes in mountaintop **observatories.** The atmosphere is thinner on mountaintops, making it easier to see far away objects in space.

The *Hubble Space Telescope* orbits Earth. It has taken many thousands of pictures.

Hubble Space Telescope

Man-made satellites and spacecraft explore the Moon. Early missions did not carry people.

LADEE Satellite

The _Lunar Atmosphere and Dust Environment Explorer_ (_LADEE_) is designed to study the Moon's thin atmosphere and the lunar dust environment.

Pictures today show detail down to single rocks. Scientists make maps of th Moon from these pictures.

Satellites in the Moon's orbit allow us to take photos of the far side of the Moon. The far side of the Moon always faces away from Earth.

Years ago, the Apollo missions landed twelve astronauts on the Moon. They collected rocks for study.

In the future, companies may launch spaceships from the Moon and explore mining. Others plan to sell tickets for Moon visits. This will add to what we know about Earth's Moon.

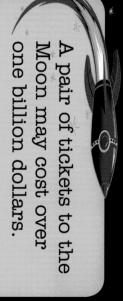

A pair of tickets to the Moon may cost over one billion dollars.

The footprints and rover tracks from the Apollo landings remain in the dust on the Moon's surface more than forty years later.

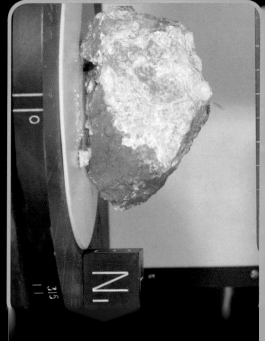

Moon rocks help us understand what the Moon is made of.

Photo Glossary

atmosphere (AT-muhs-feer): This is the layer of gases surrounding a planet.

axis (AK-siss): This invisible line runs through the center of the Moon.

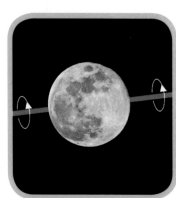

observatories (uhb-ZER-vuh-tor-eez): These are places where astronomers view outer space and its objects and collect data.

orbits (OR-bits): This describes movement in a set path around a larger object like a planet.

satellite (SAT-uh-lite): Any object that orbits Earth or another planet is a satellite. The Moon is a natural satellite.

telescopes (TELL-uh-skopes): Telescopes gather and focus light and make objects appear larger.

Index

Websites

www.nasa.gov/audience/forstudents/k-4/stories/what-is-orbit-k4.html#.
UsnAU3m76YA

http://spaceplace.nasa.gov/solar-system-formation/en/

starchild.gsfc.nasa.gov/docs/StarChild/solar_system_level1/moon.html

PHOTO CREDITS: Cover and title page © Anatolii Vasilev; page 4 © Orlo; page 5 © Keith Publicover; page 6 © muratart; page 7 © Procy; page 8 © AstroStar, page 9 © Lviatour/Images/Astronomy; page 10 and 11 © Gregory H. Revera; page 12-13 © Korionov, page 13 © BlueRingMedia; page 14 © Master3D, page 15 © Konstantin Menshikov; page 16-17 © John A Davis, page 17 © MarcelClemens; page 18 © NASA Ames and Dana Berry, page 19, 20, 21 courtesy NASA; page 22 top to bottom © Pete Pahham, Gregory H. Revera, John A Davis, page 23 top to bottom © Aphelleon, Johan Swanepoel, Master3D

Edited by Jill Sherman

Cover design and Interior design by Nicola Stratford nicolastratford.com

Library of Congress PCN Data

Moon / Julie K. Lundgren
(Inside Outer Space)
ISBN 978-1-62717-725-2 (hard cover)
ISBN 978-1-62717-847-1 (soft cover)
ISBN 978-1-62717-959-1 (e-Book)
Library of Congress Control Number: 2014935647

Rourke Educational Media
Printed in the United States of America, North Mankato, Minnesota

Also Available as:

ROURKE'S e-Books

About the Author

Julie K. Lundgren holds a deep fascination for plants, animals, and science about the natural environment. She always has great ideas for Nature Adventure Days, in which her family reluctantly participates, but then afterward they are always glad they did.

Meet The Author!
www.meetREMauthors.com